EAGLE PUBLIC LIBRARY DIST.
BOX 240 EAGLE, CO 81631
(970) 328-8800

EAGLE VALLEY LIBRARY DISTRICT

1 06 0004886792

REASONS TO CARE ABOUT

TOP 50
GIANT PANDAS

[Animals in Peril]

Mary Firestone

E
Enslow Publishers, Inc.
40 Industrial Road
Box 398
Berkeley Heights, NJ 07922
USA
http://www.enslow.com

Library of Congress Cataloguing-in-Publication Data
Top 50 reasons to care about giant pandas : animals in peril / by Mary Firestone.
    p. cm. — (Top 50 reasons to care about endangered animals)
Includes bibliographical references and index.
Summary: "Readers will learn about the giant panda's life cycle, habitat, young, diet, living in the wild and in captivity, and why it is endangered"—Provided by publisher.
ISBN 978-0-7660-3451-8
1. Giant panda—Juvenile literature. 2. Endangered species—Juvenile literature. I. Title. II. Title: Top fifty reasons to care about giant pandas.
QL737.C27F57 2010
599.789—dc22
                        2008048953

Printed in the United States of America

092009 Lake Book Manufacturing, Inc., Melrose Park, IL

10 9 8 7 6 5 4 3 2 1

To Our Readers: We have done our best to make sure all Internet Addresses in this book were active and appropriate when we went to press. However, the author and the publisher have no control over and assume no liability for the material available on those Internet sites or on other Web sites they may link to. Any comments or suggestions can be sent by e-mail to comments@enslow.com or to the address on the back cover.

♻ Enslow Publishers, Inc., is committed to printing our books on recycled paper. The paper in every book contains 10% and 30% post-consumer waste (PCW). The cover board on the outside of each book contains 100% PCW. Our goal is to do our part to help young people and the environment too!

Photographs: Jan Rysavy/iStockphoto, cover inset, 1; Jessie Cohen/AP Images, 1; Pete Oxford/Nature Picture Library, 4, 9, 49, 52, 58, 67; Bryan Faust/iStockphoto, 6; Justin Horrocks/iStockphoto, 10; iStockphoto, 13, 20, 23, 38; Red Line Editorial, 14, 54; Eric Baccega/Nature Picture Library, 17, 25, 26, 29, 41, 50, 57, 85, 99; Charles Tasnadi/AP Images, 18; Klaas Lingbeek-van Kranen/iStockphoto, 22; Jason Mooy/iStockphoto, 30; Keren Su/Corbis, 31; Jonathan Wilson/iStockphoto, 32; Joanna Pecha/iStockphoto, 33; Gavin Maxwell/Nature Picture Library, 34, 37, 45, 76, 82; Lynn M. Stone/Nature Picture Library, 42, 53; Bert van Wijk/iStockphoto, 46; Michael Chen/iStockphoto, 47, 61; Sondra Paulson/iStockphoto, 48; AP Images, 62, 73, 81, 86; Alexander Briel Perez/iStockphoto, 64 (top); Sawayasu Tsuji/iStockphoto, 64 (bottom); Beti Gorse/iStockphoto, 68; Jiaxi Shen/iStockphoto, 69; Ron Edmonds/AP Images, 70; Robert Churchill/iStockphoto, 74; Brent Reeves/iStockphoto, 78; Roman Kobzarev/iStockphoto, 79; David Longstreath/AP Images, 89; Alejandro Pagni/AP Images, 90; Liane Matrisch/iStockphoto, 93; Charlene Wittstock/AP Images, 94; Zhou Junxiang/AP Images, 97

Cover caption: A panda mother, Mei Xiang, and her cub, Tai Shan, at the National Zoo in Washington DC. Jessie Cohen/AP Images

CONTENTS

ENDANGERED PANDAS

One hundred years ago, giant pandas were plentiful in the wild. They roamed freely in many parts of Asia, including China. But in the past fifty years, pandas have been steadily disappearing. An increasing human population is the biggest cause of their disappearance. China now has a population of more than 1 billion people. These people need homes to live in and roads for traveling and getting to work. They need farms to grow food and raise livestock. These homes, roads, and farms now exist on the land that once belonged only to pandas.

Other human activities, such as poaching, are linked to panda declines. Poaching is the illegal killing of animals. Poachers kill animals such as pandas, tigers, and elephants because people buy the animals' body parts for large sums of money.

With its cuddly appearance and peaceful nature, the giant panda is one of the world's best-loved animals. Today, the panda is an international symbol of wildlife conservation. Even with all of its recognition, the panda still needs our help to prevent extinction. New laws, education, conservation techniques, and sanctuaries are leading the way.

◀ HUMAN POPULATION GROWTH IN CHINA DECREASES PANDAS' LIVING SPACE.

REASON TO CARE # 1

Pandas Eat Bamboo

High in the mountains of China's Sichuan Province, a giant panda sits in a vast thicket of bamboo. In one paw, it holds a cluster of bamboo branches. The panda pulls off the leaves with the other paw and eats them. It removes the bamboo bark with its teeth.

If there is not enough bamboo, a panda will eat other plants, such as irises or clover. A panda spends much of its time eating. It will take the panda all day to eat its fill.

[A panda eats not only bamboo branches, but also bamboo leaves, shoots, and stems. The leaves are the easiest part for the panda's stomach to digest.]

◀ PANDAS DEPEND ON BAMBOO TO SURVIVE.

Panda Means the "Great Bear-Cat" in Chinese

Thousands of years ago, the Chinese took note of an unusual black and white creature roaming in the mountains near Tibet. Today, English speakers call it the giant panda. The Chinese call the panda the *daxiongmao*, the "great bear-cat."

Westerners first became aware of giant pandas in 1869. Scientists studied the panda, eventually giving it its scientific name *Ailuropoda melanoleuca*. It is a Latin name that classifies the panda with bears. It means "cat-footed black and white" animal.

[An ancestor of the giant panda, *Ailurarctos*, is an extinct genus of Chinese panda that lived 8 million years ago. The skull of another ancestor, *Ailuropoda microta*, shows that it was about half the size that pandas are today.]

▶ A PANDA EXPLORES ITS CHINESE HABITAT.

REASON TO CARE # 3

Pandas Are a Threatened Species

The International Union for Conservation of Nature (IUCN) Red List of Threatened Species is the most widely recognized listing of animal conservation statuses. Giant pandas are listed as endangered on the Red List.

The term endangered describes an animal's conservation status. A conservation status is given to a species when it has been observed by scientists over a long period of time. Scientists keep track of any increases and decreases in the animal's populations.

[In the past, hunters from around the world came to China to kill the giant panda for trophies. Scientists and researchers also killed pandas to learn more about them. These practices contributed to the panda's endangered status.]

◀ IN THE PAST, PANDAS WERE HUNTED FOR THEIR FUR.

Pandas Are a Flagship Species

Pandas are called a flagship species because they draw attention to the cause of animal conservation through their unique behaviors or appearance. In some ways, they are representatives for other species. Preserving pandas helps other animals and forms of wildlife that share their habitats by bringing attention to them.

[Along with pandas, other flagship species include marine turtles, great apes, and polar bears.]

► SAVING PANDAS CAN HELP SAVE OTHER ANIMALS THAT SHARE THEIR HABITATS.

CHINA

SICHUAN GIANT
PANDA SANCTUARIES

INDIAN
OCEAN

Panda Sanctuaries Protect Endangered Animals

About one-third of the world's pandas live in the Sichuan Giant Panda Sanctuaries, which are located in the Qionglai and Jiajin mountains of central China. The sanctuaries have seven nature reserves and nine wildlife parks and cover a huge expanse of land: 2,283 acres (924 hectares). In these protected places, the giant panda shares life with other endangered species, such as the snow leopard, the red panda, and the clouded leopard.

[The sanctuaries of Sichuan Province are in one of the world's richest botanical sites.]

◀ THE SICHUAN GIANT PANDA SANCTUARIES IN CHINA HELP PROTECT PANDAS.

Baby Pandas Are Born in Natural Reserves

The Wolong National Nature Reserve is the largest panda reserve in China. It is located in the Sichuan Province and is the most famous among the Sichuan sanctuaries. The Chinese government works with the World Wildlife Fund (WWF) to create a breeding center for pandas at the reserve.

In May 2008, a large earthquake displaced many pandas at Wolong. They were moved to the Bifeng Gorge Base of China Panda Protection and Research Center.

[Wolong National Nature Reserve is one of several panda reserves in China. The Chinese government has established more than fifty panda reserves.]

▶ RESEARCHERS HOLD FIVE-MONTH-OLD PANDA BABIES AT THE WOLONG RESERVE.

Pandas
Experience Stress

The first pandas in the United States were Ling-Ling and Hsing-Hsing. They were able to produce offspring at the National Zoo in Washington DC, but the cubs did not survive beyond a few weeks. Unfortunately, Ling-Ling and Hsing-Hsing's difficulties were common to other pandas that had tried to mate and raise their young in captivity. Experts discovered that pandas, especially males, experience a lot of stress when they are kept for long periods in small areas. Pandas prefer to live away from people, and they live alone in nature as adults.

Sanctuaries in China have enough open range areas for pandas, and they have been able to breed very successfully there.

◀ LING-LING AND HSING-HSING PLAY AT THE NATIONAL ZOO IN 1974.

REASON TO CARE # 8

Pandas Are Shaped Like Other Bears

Pandas are usually between 4 and 6 feet (1.2 to 1.8 meters) long. A full-grown panda can weigh 165 to 350 pounds (75 to 160 kilograms). Their shape is very similar to that of other bears, which means their bodies are round in the middle. Pandas have a short, wide tail and a large, round head.

[Pandas have plantigrade feet. This means that the entire foot—toes and heel—touch the ground when walking. This is similar to the way humans, other bears, and many rodents walk. Other animals, such as dogs, cats, or horses, walk with their weight on their toes.]

◀ PANDAS' PLANTIGRADE FEET MEAN THEY ARE SLOW WALKERS.

Some Pandas Look Like Raccoons

Although the red panda shares a name with the giant panda, it is more closely related to weasels and skunks. It is also called the lesser panda, and is much smaller than the giant panda. Its features resemble a raccoon. It has reddish brown fur with a black lower section and a long, fluffy, striped tail.

▼ RED PANDAS LOOK LIKE RACCOONS.

▲ RED PANDAS HAVE STRIPED TAILS AND "MASKS" AROUND THEIR EYES, LIKE THIS RACCOON.

Red pandas weigh about 7 to 20 pounds (3 to 9 kilograms). Red pandas live in the mountains of China. Like giant pandas, they eat bamboo, but they also like berries, acorns, and bird eggs.

Bamboo is actually a grass. There are more than seven hundred kinds of bamboo.

Bamboo Is a Large Part of a Panda's Diet

Wild pandas live almost entirely on bamboo. They will occasionally eat fish and small rodents. Still, bamboo makes up between 95 and 99 percent of their daily diet. Long ago, pandas were carnivores that ate meat, but over time they have come to live mostly on bamboo. There are several hundred types of bamboo. Pandas eat many varieties, but they have two favorites: arrow bamboo and umbrella bamboo.

Because their digestive systems were made for meat, pandas do not take in nutrients easily from their purely vegetarian diet. Pandas must eat an enormous amount of bamboo to meet their dietary needs. Bamboo does not have a high nutritional value, so an adult panda eats between 25 and 80 pounds of bamboo each day, including the leaves, stalks, and young shoots.

[Bamboo leaves contain a lot of protein and also provide the panda with a source of water. There are twenty-five bamboo species that pandas eat, but only a few are abundant in the mountains where they live.]

▶ A PANDA MUNCHES ON A STALK OF BAMBOO.

REASON TO CARE # 11

Pandas Have Strong Stomachs

Even though pandas were carnivores in their distant past, they have adapted somewhat to the diet of an herbivore. The lining of the panda's esophagus is tough, which protects it from the bamboo splinters. The panda's stomach has strong muscles to help digest the woody pieces of bamboo. Thick jaw muscles enable pandas to crush stiff bamboo stalks. Huge, smooth molars toward the back of the panda's mouth help grind the stalks to tiny pieces. But pandas lack the chemicals in their bodies that herbivores have to digest plants such as bamboo. A panda's body eliminates most of the bamboo branches and leaves that it eats before the food is digested. Pandas have to eat a lot of bamboo to get the nutrients they need.

[The esophagus is the tube of muscle that carries the food from the mouth to the stomach.]

◀ PANDAS HAVE VERY STRONG TEETH TO HELP THEM CHEW TOUGH FOODS.

Pandas Have Thick Coats

Pandas have adapted well to their cool-weather homes in the mountains of China. Even as they roll around and walk through thick patches of snow, pandas spend winters comfortably because their coats protect them. A panda's thick fur is coarse to the touch and covered with an oily substance that prevents cold and moisture from reaching the skin. Beneath the coarse outer layer of fur is a soft underlayer. This layer holds the panda's body heat close to the surface of the skin, which also protects the panda from the cold.

▶ PANDA FUR IS WARM AND ALLOWS THE PANDA TO LIVE IN COLD CLIMATES.

Catlike Eyes Help Pandas See in the Dark

Two large black patches around the panda's eyes create its distinctive look. Panda eyes have vertical slit-shaped pupils similar to a cat's eyes.

Pandas frequently wake up in the middle of the night to eat. Even though their eyesight is generally poor, their pupils help them during night feeding. Their unique pupils expand to let in more of the available light, which helps them see in the dark.

▼ A PANDA IS EASILY RECOGNIZED BY THE BLACK PATCHES AROUND ITS EYES.

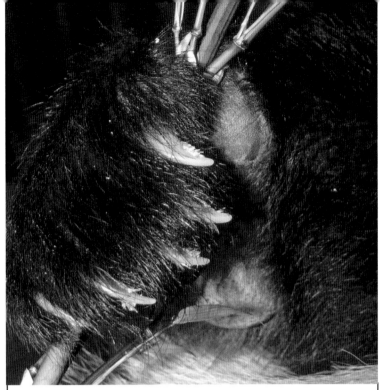

▲ PANDAS HAVE "THUMBS" THAT ALLOW THEM TO GRASP BAMBOO.

REASON TO CARE # 14

Paws and Claws Help Pandas Eat

The panda's front and back paws have five toes and thick pads. On each wrist, a panda has a padded bone that functions like a thumb. This false thumb comes in handy for holding and scraping leaves off bamboo stalks. Pandas also have long, sharp claws that allow them to climb swiftly up trees.

Pandas Have Sharp Teeth

Like other members of the bear family, the panda has between thirty-two and forty-two teeth, including sharp canines. These teeth make it possible for pandas to break up bamboo to get to the pith (the spongy tissue inside plants).

▼ A PANDA USES ITS CLAWS AND TEETH TO TEAR THROUGH THICK BAMBOO.

▲ PANDAS HAVE SHARP CANINE TEETH.

Pandas also have an excellent sense of smell and large ears with excellent hearing. Because pandas like to live alone, they use their sense of smell to avoid meeting other pandas. But when it is time to mate, male pandas use their sense of smell to find females.

[Canine teeth are the four pointed upper and lower teeth on the sides of the mouth.]

REASON TO CARE # 16

Pandas Blend Into Snowy Environments

With its striking black and white markings, it seems that the panda would be easy to spot in any environment. However, some experts believe the opposite: that the marks developed over time to act as a camouflage. In its natural habitat, the panda's high contrast markings break up its outline in the forest, making it hard for predators to tell exactly where or what the panda is, especially in a snowy forest environment.

◀ A PANDA'S MARKINGS FUNCTION AS A CAMOUFLAGE TO HELP IT HIDE FROM PREDATORS.

Pandas Are
Born in Dens

Pregnant pandas find a hollow tree where they can give birth. Some pandas make their dens in caves. They line it with branches and bamboo. After a pregnancy that averages four and a half months, the panda will go to the den and give birth to one or two cubs. The mother panda will not leave her den for an entire week while she tends to the needs of her newborn. She licks the cub and keeps it close to her. The cub nurses regularly on the milk from the mother panda.

[Mother pandas in captivity give birth to twins more often than mothers in the wild. When a mother panda gives birth to two cubs in the wild, she will only raise one cub. Scientists say the mother is ensuring that at least one of her offspring survives in case there is not enough food in the habitat. But survival of even a single cub is challenging. More than half of newborn pandas die from diseases or from being accidentally crushed by their mothers.]

▶ A PANDA DEN IN THE QUINLING MOUNTAINS OF CHINA

REASON TO CARE # 18

A Baby Panda's Eyes Are Sealed Shut

A panda cub is 6 inches (15 centimeters) long when it is born, and it weighs only 4 ounces (113 grams). With just a light coat of white fur and pink skin showing through it, a cub does not look like a panda at first. But a cub begins to develop dark patches around its eyes in about one week. A baby panda's tail is relatively long when it is first born, and its eyes are sealed shut. A cub's eyes open at six weeks of age.

Cubs grow quickly during their first two months of life. One panda born at the San Diego Zoo weighed 6.5 pounds (3 kilograms) after eight weeks.

◄ A NEWBORN PANDA RESTS INSIDE AN INCUBATOR AT A PANDA RESEARCH CENTER.

Panda Cubs First Walk at Three Months Old

At three weeks old, cubs have dark patches and white fur like their parents. Their fur is still very soft. When they are six weeks old, they can crawl. At three to four months, a panda cub takes its first steps. At this stage of development, pandas weigh around 22 pounds (10 kilograms).

[Baby pandas nurse on their mothers' milk for eight to nine months.]

▶ A THREE-WEEK-OLD BABY PANDA IS CARED FOR IN A CHINESE CONSERVATION CENTER.

PANDA BEHAVIOR

Pandas Communicate with Barks and Growls

Pandas growl when they want to scare away other animals. They also lower their heads to stare at their opponents. Female pandas bark loudly when they want to attract a mate. Male pandas let out a loud bark when they see a potential mate. When a panda is frightened, it often covers its eyes with its paws until the feeling passes. If a panda is standing on its hind legs, it is making itself look larger to appear more threatening.

◄ PANDAS COMMUNICATE BY RAISING AND LOWERING THEIR HEADS.

Scents Help Pandas Mark Their Territories

Pandas live alone in the wild unless they are raising cubs. Like many other wild animals, pandas stake out personal territories known as home ranges. They claim these areas as their own by leaving scent marks with urine and droppings of feces. Pandas also produce a strong-smelling substance from a gland located under their tails, which they rub on rocks, trees, and leaves. A panda might even do a handstand to leave a scent mark higher up a tree's trunk. All of these behaviors let visitors know they are walking on claimed territory.

▶ PANDAS LEAVE SCRATCHES ON TREES TO MARK THEIR TERRITORIES.

Pandas Spend Many Hours a Day Eating

Pandas live out in the open. Unless it is a mother with cubs, a panda does not have a cave that it returns to each night. But pandas need a place to rest after wandering around and eating. Pandas often sleep under trees, in hollow trees, in caves, and on rocks. They spend at least half of their days searching for food and eating—sometimes up to sixteen hours. They spend the rest of the time sleeping.

▼ A PANDA RESTS.

▲ PANDAS SPEND MUCH OF THEIR TIME SEARCHING FOR
FOOD AND EATING.

Pandas eat in the early morning hours, at dusk, and during the night. This means they spend most of the daylight hours sleeping.

[A panda's diet prevents it from storing fat like other bears, so it cannot hibernate in the winter.]

Zoo Pandas Eat
More Than Bamboo

Pandas in zoos eat a lot of bamboo. Some zoos feed each panda more than 50 pounds (23 kilograms) of bamboo each day. But captive pandas also eat a nourishing mixture of carrots, apples, rice, and honey. They also eat special biscuits, which have vitamins added.

▼ THIS PANDA EATS CLOVER AND OTHER GRASSES.

▲ PANDAS PLAY TOGETHER BEFORE THEY MATE.

REASON TO CARE # 24

Female Pandas Bleat and Bark

To attract a male, the female panda releases a unique scent, broadcasting that she is ready to mate. She also bleats and barks. Nearby males hear her calls and sometimes fight with each other to become her mate. In the end, one male panda manages to chase all of his competitors away. Before mating, the male and female pandas play together. However, after mating is complete, the female panda will chase the male out of her territory.

REASON TO CARE # 25

Mother Pandas Teach Their Cubs to Find Food

When a cub is four weeks old, it cannot walk, crawl, or see. At six weeks, the mother panda takes the cub with her as she searches for bamboo. By this time, the cub can wiggle and roll. The mother panda must carry her cub wherever she goes. When a cub is able to walk, it follows its mother while she looks for bamboo to eat. On these walks, the cub learns how to mark trees and recognize the scents of other pandas. Panda cubs begin eating bamboo when they are five or six months old, but they continue to receive milk from their mothers.

When out with their mothers, panda cubs climb trees. Trees provide young pandas with a safe place to nap and hide from predators. Panda cubs are very playful. They like to climb on their mothers, roll around, slide down hills, and lie in grass.

◀ A MOTHER PANDA HOLDS HER CUB IN THE WOLONG RESERVE IN CHINA.

Pandas
Leave Home

Pandas leave the safety of their mothers when they are around eighteen months old. Some stay in their mother's home range for a little while. Then, the grown cubs go out to establish their own territories.

▼ A GROUP OF YOUNG PANDAS CLIMB TOGETHER IN THE WOLONG RESERVE IN CHINA.

▲ MOST PANDAS LIVE SOLITARY LIVES.

REASON TO CARE # 27

Adult Pandas
Live Alone

When a panda reaches adulthood, it spends its days roaming through the forest alone. One of the most important things to a panda is finding the best bamboo patches. Adult pandas like forest areas with many old hollow pine trees that can provide shelter. They seek areas with several species of bamboo. Female pandas stay close to the type of bamboo they like best, while male pandas wander more.

CHINA

BURMA
(MYANMAR)

VIETNAM

INDIAN
OCEAN

 PANDA RANGE

PANDA HABITATS

REASON TO CARE # 28

Panda Populations Are Declining

A habitat is an area of land that provides everything an animal needs to survive and raise its young. A habitat has enough food, water, and shelter for the animal.

Giant pandas were once abundant in southern and eastern China. They also lived in China's neighboring nations, Vietnam and Burma (also known as Myanmar). Today, the giant panda can only be found in fragmented regions of central China.

◀ PANDAS ONCE FLOURISHED IN SOUTHERN AND EASTERN CHINA.

Pandas Prefer a Cool Environment

Pandas live among deciduous, coniferous, and bamboo forests high in the mountains of central China. In previous centuries, pandas also made their homes in low-lying river basins, but loss of habitat has pushed the species higher into the mountains. This is where bamboo, their main food source, is still plentiful.

The panda's mountain habitat in China is known for its misty, cool weather. This is the panda's preferred climate. The pandas make their homes near rivers and streams. Panda habitat has been reduced to a 5,000-square-mile area of mountains in China.

▶ PANDAS LIKE TO LIVE IN COOL CLIMATES.

Scientists Use Radio Collars to Track Pandas

Radio collaring is one way to track a panda's daily travels. To attach a radio collar to a panda, scientists shoot a dart from a gun. The dart injects a tranquilizer into the panda, which causes the animal to sleep for a short time. Scientists quickly fit the panda with a radio collar that sends out radio signals. A receiver picks up the signals. By keeping track of a panda's movements, the scientists can observe a panda's range.

◀ SCIENTISTS WORK TO UNDERSTAND HOW PANDAS LIVE.

Bamboo Corridors
Extend Panda Habitats

Fragmented habitats make life difficult for pandas in two ways. Pandas depend on bamboo for a main food source. But bamboo grows in intervals. Because of the life cycle of bamboo, sometimes an entire bamboo forest will die completely, leaving pandas without a food source. To find more food, pandas search in new territories. But when their ranges are broken apart by farms, highways, and towns, they cannot reach these areas. These pandas could end up starving. Fragmented habitats also affect panda breeding by preventing panda diversity.

Bamboo corridors will soon change these problems. The Chinese government is working with the World Wildlife Fund (WWF) to link isolated pockets of panda habitats with corridors of bamboo forest. Through the creation of bamboo corridors that link habitats, the panda's range will be greatly extended. This makes more food available and also helps the panda's genetic diversity and population growth.

▶ BAMBOO CORRIDORS CAN HELP PANDAS SURVIVE IN THE WILD.

REASON TO CARE # 32

Infrared Cameras Tell Scientists About Pandas

The Wanglang Nature Reserve in China's Sichuan Province has installed forty infrared cameras in the trees of panda habitats. Triggered by the movement of any passing animal, the cameras take pictures of pandas and other wildlife sharing their habitat. These cameras help scientists keep a more accurate estimate of how many pandas are living in the wild.

[The Wanglang Nature Reserve has been supported by the World Wildlife Fund (WWF) since 1996.]

◀ A CHINESE SCIENTIST HELPS A SICK PANDA IN CHINA'S SICHUAN PROVINCE.

PANDAS IN CULTURE

REASON TO CARE # 33

Pandas Symbolize Harmony

Many Chinese place much importance on the philosophy that the universe is made of two opposing forces: Yin and Yang. One symbol of Yin and Yang is a circle with one white half and one black half.

The giant panda in Chinese culture is a symbol of this philosophy, with its black and white fur parts standing out in high contrast to each other. The Chinese say the gentle nature of the panda demonstrates how the Yin and Yang in nature bring peace and harmony when they are in balance.

◄ TOP: YIN AND YANG SYMBOLIZE OPPOSING FORCES.
BOTTOM: PANDAS ARE A SYMBOL OF HARMONY.

Pandas Are Part of Chinese History

Members of an ancient Chinese people from the Xizhou Dynasty (1027–771 B.C.) wrote down all of their customs and beliefs in a text called the *Shangshu*. This text described the giant panda as an invincible creature with great physical power. Other writings from that time repeat this notion of panda strength. Even though the panda was known by ancient cultures to be strong, it was also known for its gentleness. The people from Pingwu, China, recognized that pandas never hurt people or other animals. In China the panda became a national symbol of peace.

[Centuries ago, warring tribes would raise a flag with an image of a panda on it to stop a battle or to call a truce.]

▶ PANDAS ARE A SYMBOL OF PEACE.

Pandas Have Many Names

Over the centuries, the Chinese people have given the panda several names. The earliest writings referred to the panda as *pi* and *pixiu*. Additional names followed. Some of these names mean "beast of prey," "white leopard," "iron-eating beast," and "bamboo bear."

▼ PANDA NAMES SOMETIMES DESCRIBE THEIR PHYSICAL APPEARANCE.

▲ PANDAS HAVE BEEN CALLED BAMBOO BEAR.

Today, the Chinese have other names for the panda. Some of them mean "banded bear," "catlike bear," "bearlike cat," or "great bear-cat."

[The word *panda* may have developed from the Nepalese word *poonya*, which means "bamboo-" or "plant-eating animal."]

REASON TO CARE # 36

The Chinese Government Gave Pandas as Gifts

Diplomacy is a type of negotiating process. World leaders often use diplomacy to improve relationships with other nations and demonstrate goodwill. Panda diplomacy is a famous term that began when China started giving pandas as diplomatic gifts to other countries. The Chinese began this practice long ago, during the Tang Dynasty (618–907 A.D.), when Empress Wu Zetian sent two pandas to the emperor of Japan.

When Richard Nixon was president of the United States in 1972, he visited China. He was the first U.S. president to ever visit that country. Upon his return to the United States, he received two pandas from the Chinese leader, Chairman Mao. Ling-Ling and Hsing-Hsing were placed in the National Zoo in Washington DC. More than 1 million people visited them during their first year there.

[In 1974, China gave England two pandas: Ching-Ching and Chia-Chia.]

◄ HSING-HSING WAS A GIFT TO THE UNITED STATES FROM CHINESE CHAIRMAN MAO.

Panda Fur Is Warm and Waterproof

Panda fur is valued for being warm, waterproof, and good for bedding. An ancient Chinese belief that panda skin has magic powers remains today. The tradition says that sleeping on a panda skin will scare away ghosts. Some people also believe that the practice will predict the future in dreams. These beliefs contribute to the problem of poaching. Killing pandas is illegal and has very serious consequences for the poachers when they are caught. Poachers continue to take the risk because a single panda skin is worth thousands of dollars on the black market.

It has been illegal to kill pandas in China since the 1960s, but the laws were not strictly enforced. Poachers continued to kill pandas, so the Chinese government made stricter laws in 1987. The new laws increased punishment from two years to a much more severe sentence. A poacher could be sent to prison for life or even be put to death. Today, the punishment is less severe: ten to twenty years in prison.

► THESE PANDAS WERE KILLED BY POACHERS WHO WERE ARRESTED. THE FURS WERE GIVEN TO A MUSEUM.

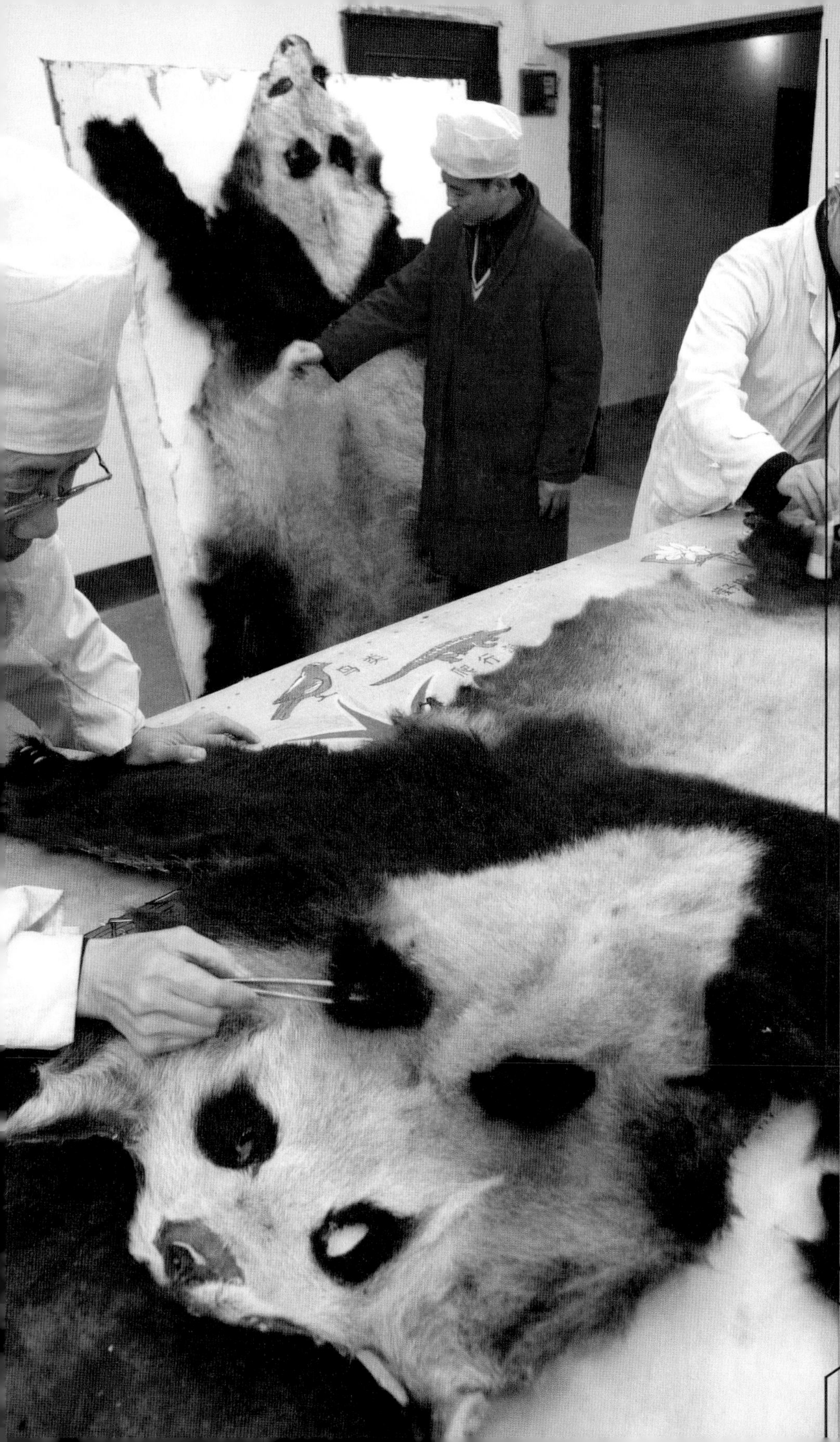

THREATS TO PANDAS

REASON TO CARE # 38

Bamboo Dieback Threatens Pandas

Today, between 1,000 and 3,000 giant pandas live in the wild, but many groups believe there are fewer than 1,600. Pandas have been given a threatened status because the increasing human population makes it difficult for pandas to sustain their populations.

A main cause of panda loss is bamboo dieback. Bamboo plants grow from a small shoot to a thick stalk as high as 164 feet, depending on the type. They continue to produce stalks and leaves until the bamboo plant flowers and dies. This can cause problems for pandas living in that area, because they need bamboo to survive. With flowering intervals lasting fifteen to one hundred thirty years, species of bamboo forests die off completely. It can take ten or more years before bamboo grows back. Pandas also lose habitat when humans cut down bamboo to clear space for land development.

◄ BAMBOO DIEBACK IS A LARGE THREAT TO PANDA SURVIVAL.

REASON TO CARE # 39

Pandas Are Losing Their Habitats

Steadily over the last century, the giant panda has lost its habitat because of a growing human population. However, people need land for farms, livestock, and homes. Forest-based industries provide jobs and boost local economies. The answer to the problem of habitat loss is not easy, and sadly, wild pandas are left only with fragments of their formerly vast territories.

[The giant panda's habitat forms the watershed for the Yangtze and Yellow Rivers of China. More than 500 million people live in this area.]

◄ POPULATION GROWTH IN CHINA IS A THREAT TO PANDA SURVIVAL.

Panda Cubs Are
Vulnerable to Predators

Pandas are large and strong. They do not have any real predators in the wild, but their cubs are vulnerable. Mother pandas keep very close track of their cubs. If given the chance, animals such as snow leopards will prey on panda cubs for food. But panda cubs are good climbers, and some are able to escape by climbing trees.

▼ PANDA CUBS ARE THREATENED BY PREDATORS.

▲ SOME SNOW LEOPARDS PREY ON PANDA CUBS.

The biggest threat to pandas is human beings, who have hunted them for their pelts and fragmented their habitats.

[Snow leopards are also an endangered species. Loss of habitat for the snow leopard has also reduced populations of their natural prey—wild goats and sheep. This makes panda cubs more vulnerable to snow leopards, which wander into panda territories looking for food.]

Logging Destroys Panda Habitats

The logging industry in China has caused a significant loss of forest areas and panda habitat. In 1998, China's government banned commercial logging in the nation's southwestern area to protect pandas. The World Wildlife Fund (WWF) has been working with people in Pingwu County, Sichuan Province. They have been teaching logging businesses how to conserve habitats while still using forest resources.

[The logging industry produces timber, or lumber. This wood is used to build homes, furniture, and flooring. Wood is also used to make paper, pencils, and many other everyday products.]

▶ THE LOGGING INDUSTRY HAS CUT INTO FORESTED AREAS WHERE PANDAS LIVE.

Pandas Are Hurt by Hunting Traps

When pandas wander through the forests looking for food, they are sometimes accidentally caught in traps that were set for other animals. Hunters set traps for deer, bears, and other large animals. Pandas are hurt and sometimes killed by these traps. On reserves, rangers patrol to watch for poachers and for pandas that have been caught in traps.

As human populations grow, pandas and humans come into closer contact. As their habitats become more fragmented, pandas are forced to travel farther to find sufficient food. This makes pandas more vulnerable to starvation if they are not able to reach new habitats safely to find food.

◀ BECAUSE OF HUMAN POPULATION GROWTH, PANDAS MUST TRAVEL FARTHER TO FIND FOOD.

REASON TO CARE # 43

Small Territories Lead to Panda Inbreeding

Loss of habitat has led to smaller territories for pandas. This creates a problem for pandas trying to find new mates. With fewer mates to choose from, pandas end up mating with partners who are closely related to them. This is called inbreeding. Inbreeding leaves pandas vulnerable to diseases and sometimes causes pandas to be unable to have cubs of their own.

▶ INBREEDING CAN CAUSE PANDAS TO BE UNABLE TO REPRODUCE.

PANDA CONSERVATION

Scientists Train Pandas to Survive in the Wild

Introducing giant pandas back into the wild is an important part of China's efforts to save them over the long term. It takes a lot of training, however, to teach a panda to live in the wild after it has been in captivity.

On February 19, 2007, Chinese scientists found the dead body of Xiang Xiang, a panda that had been raised in captivity and released into the wild. They believed that the panda died from falling from a high place after fighting with other animals.

The panda had been released into the wild in April 2006. Xiang Xiang had been trained on how to survive in the wild, including how to build a den and mark his territory. After finding the panda's body and determining the cause of death, scientists realized areas in which the program needs to improve in order to be successful.

◀ CROWDS WATCH AS XIANG XIANG IS RELEASED INTO THE WILD IN APRIL 2006.

Ecotourism Raises Money for Pandas

If you want to get close to pandas in the wild, someday you might go to China and stay at Panda Mountain. In 2008, Panda Mountain announced plans to be in business as an ecotourism destination. Panda Mountain will use the money it makes from tourism to support the Wolong Panda and Conservation Institute. Pandas and other wildlife share the reserve land with five thousand indigenous peoples, who also benefit from the tourism. When they receive financial support from tourism, they do not have to rely on illegal trade and poaching to survive.

While ecotourism provides more income for reserves, conservationists say that it can also make matters worse for the animal habitats. The transportation used by the tourists might cause pollution. Tourists also eat food, use energy for cooking, and leave waste products behind.

[Ecotourism is visiting natural environments in a way that affects the ecology as little as possible.]

▶ ECOTOURISM CAN PROVIDE MONEY FOR NATURE RESERVES.

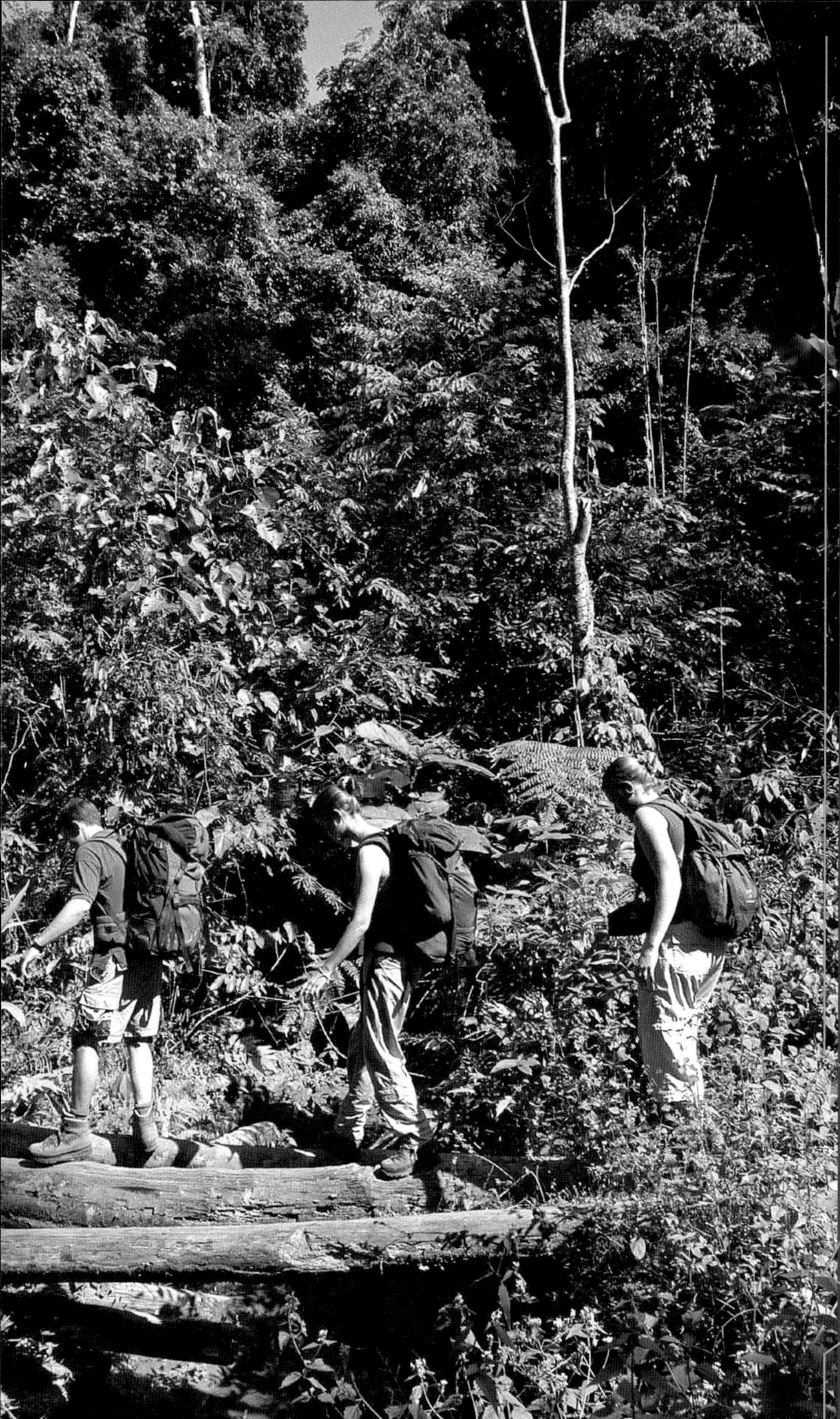

REASON TO CARE # 46

Adoption
Helps Pandas

Saving giant pandas costs money, and conservationists need all the help they can get. The World Wildlife Fund (WWF) has created the Adopt a Panda Program to provide a way for people to participate in this valuable work. Participants can register at the Adopt a Panda link on the WWF Web site. For a small donation, members receive a panda adoption certificate and a color photo of the panda they are supporting.

Another panda adoption program is available at Pandas International. Classrooms of students raise money and adopt pandas as a group with the help of their teachers. Their adoptions include regular updates on a panda's progress, certificates, newsletters, and other items.

◀ THE PANDA IS THE SYMBOL OF THE WORLD WILDLIFE FUND.

Sustainable Energy Protects Panda Forests

Cutting down forests is not limited to the logging industry. People living in or near panda habitats burn lumber to keep warm and to cook food. This additional loss of forest habitat has had a big impact on panda survival.

To conserve the trees and panda habitat, the WWF is providing local people with energy efficient stoves and biogas. Many people in mountain areas of China keep pigs. Biogas is created when the pig manure is turned into methane gas. This is a sustainable energy source that helps save forests. Another program teaches beekeeping as a means for earning an income without affecting forests.

▶ BIOGAS PLANTS HELP CREATE SUSTAINABLE ENERGY.

REASON TO CARE # 48

The WWF Raises Money for Pandas

The WWF became involved in giant panda conservation in China in 1980. In recent years, it has been working with the government of China in its National Conservation Programme for the Giant Panda and its Habitat. The group has trained staff at nature reserves and government workers on how to control poaching, monitor wildlife, and involve local communities in the fight for conservation. The WWF also supports fund-raisers and events that raise awareness for panda conservation.

[The giant panda has a special significance for the WWF. It has been the organization's symbol since the group formed in 1961.]

◀ A MODEL POSES WITH A PANDA GOWN AT A 2008 WWF FUND-RAISER IN SINGAPORE.

The WWF Helps
Stop Illegal Poaching

When the logging industry was banned in China in the 1990s, many rural people were left without a means to survive. They turned to hunting wildlife and poaching to create and sell traditional Chinese medicines illegally.

The WWF has worked with the Chinese government to find alternative sources of income for these people. Through government channels, the WWF provided Chinese citizens access to Carrefour, a hypermarket. Carrefour combines a supermarket and a department store. This connection helps rural Chinese find a market for legal goods such as honey, walnuts, and tea.

▶ CUSTOMERS SHOP AT CARREFOUR IN SHANGHAI, CHINA.

You Can Help Save Pandas

Fun and Rewarding Ways to Help Save Pandas

- Go to your school library and read about pandas and other forms of wildlife.
- Share your knowledge with others. Tell your friends and family about the conservation of wildlife and how people have an impact on the environment.
- Start an Adopt a Panda program at your school. Ask your school to participate.
- Join a conservation group, such as the WWF. These groups offer membership materials, such as magazines and gifts. The profits are used to help panda conservation efforts.
- Help your class plan a fund-raiser to support an organization that protects pandas.
- Search the Internet for wildlife conservation groups, zoos in your area, and information about pandas. Some Web sites have videos of pandas in the wild and in captivity.
- Begin a wildlife conservation science project. Create posters and share video clips to educate your community about pandas.

▶ YOU CAN HELP SAVE PANDAS!

GLOSSARY

black market—The business of selling illegal products, such as body parts of endangered animals.

botanical—Relating to plant life.

camouflage—A way of hiding or blending into the background.

canines—The four cone-shaped, pointed teeth of the upper and lower jaw.

carnivore—An animal that eats meat.

coniferous—Having needles or scale-like leaves.

conservation—The protection of nature and animals.

corridors—A narrow tract of land that forms a passageway.

deciduous—Having leaves that fall off seasonally.

dynasty—A sequence of rulers from the same family.

endangered—At risk of becoming extinct.

extinct—Died out completely.

forest-based industry—Any industry that relies on wood products for income, such as construction companies and paper mills.

genus—A group of related animals, often made up of many species.

herbivore—An animal that eats only plants.

inbreeding—Mating between two individuals that are too closely related.

manure—Any animal or plant material used to fertilize land, especially animal feces.

molar—A tooth in the back of the mouth used for grinding food.

Nepalese—The language spoken in Nepal, a nation located in the Himalayas between India and Tibet.

pith—The soft, spongy center of bamboo.

population—The total number of a group of animals.

reserve—A protected area for animals to live.

species—A specific group of animals with shared physical characteristics and genes; members within a species can breed with each other to produce offspring.

sustainable—Able to be renewed.

territory—An area defended by one animal against others.

watershed—A region draining into a river system or other body of water.

Books

Bortolotti, Dan. *Panda Rescue: Changing the Future for Endangered Wildlife.* Buffalo, NY: Firefly, 2003.

Lindburg, Donald, and Karen Baragona, eds. *Giant Pandas: Biology and Conservation.* Berkeley, CA: University of California Press, 2004.

Mackay, Richard. *The Atlas of Endangered Species.* Berkeley, CA: University of California Press, 2008.

McGavin, George C. *Endangered: Wildlife on the Brink of Extinction.* Buffalo, NY: Firefly, 2006.

Seidensticker, John, and Susan Lumpkin. *Smithsonian Book of Giant Pandas.* Washington, DC: Smithsonian, 2002.

Internet Addresses

Pandas International
<http://www.pandasinternational.org/panda_party.html>

The Smithsonian—Giant Pandas
<http://nationalzoo.si.edu/Animals/GiantPandas/MeetPandas/default.cfm>

World Wildlife Fund
<http://www.panda.org>

INDEX